SMITHSONIAN EXPLORES

BUGS & INSECTS

Discover the Fascinating World of Creepy Crawly Creatures!

Jane Parks Gardner

weldonowen

CONTENTS

INTRODUCTION

Creepy, crawly, and completely amazing—welcome to the wild world of insects!

From shimmering dragonflies that ruled the skies long before dinosaurs roamed the planet, to beetles strong enough to lift more than eight hundred times their own weight, insects are some of the most fascinating creatures on Earth.

With millions of species around the world, these tiny animals live on land, in water, and even inside plants. They buzz, leap, glow, sting, and even play dead, but insects aren't just cool—they're also vital to life on our planet. Get ready to uncover their secrets, superpowers, and strange survival tricks. This is the incredible story of bugs and insects!

Chapter 1
BUTTERFLIES & MOTHS

What has six legs, two pairs of wings, and dusty scales that shimmer in light? Butterflies and moths, of course! These amazing fliers include more than 180,000 species, each with its own unique attributes. Most butterflies are bright and colorful. We often see them during the day, but some species are nocturnal, or active at night. Moths have more muted tones. We often see them at night, but some species are diurnal, or active during the day. Let's explore their incredible world!

A LIFE OF TRANSFORMATION

Butterflies go through an amazing transformation that includes four life stages.

EGG

ADULT

CATERPILLAR

CHRYSALIS

Moths go through a similar transformation, only inside a cocoon, not a chrysalis. The cocoon is spun from silk, which hardens into place to protect the life inside.

The pupa, or chrysalis, consists of a hard, sturdy exterior to protect it against weather and predators.

EGG

First, a butterfly lays its eggs on a plant.

CATERPILLAR (LARVA)

Tiny caterpillars hatch, hungry and ready to munch on leaves so they can grow.

CHRYSALIS (PUPA)

When it's time, the caterpillar hangs upside down in a safe place, among twigs or leaves, and forms a chrysalis. Inside, the caterpillar begins its wild transformation where it becomes a soupy-like texture before reorganizing its body and emerging anew.

ADULT

It can take from a few weeks to several months for the transformation to occur. When completed, the chrysalis or cocoon splits open, and out emerges a butterfly or moth, ready to take flight!

BUTTERFLY VS. MOTH

Butterflies tend to fly and glide gracefully.

Moths tend to flit and zigzag more when in flight.

Butterflies rest with their wings folded.

Many moths relax with their wings open.

A butterfly's antennae are thin with little bulbs.

Some moths have feather or saw-shaped antennae, but most have threadlike antennae without a bulb at the end.

SUPERIOR
SENSES

Male moths can detect a single molecule of a female's pheromone from miles away using their feathery antennae. Pheromones are chemicals produced by animals used to attract or signal others in the same species.

Some antennae help butterflies smell flowers—their food source—from a mile away.

Tiny sensors in their feet let them "taste" whatever they land on.

Both creatures have compound eyes that help them see 360 degrees around.

Their eyes can see ultraviolet light, which helps them detect—and avoid—dangerous predators in darkness.

Their antennae help them navigate, detect danger, and react to changes in temperatures.

Butterflies and moths have a proboscis: a tube that acts like a straw to help them sip nectar, tree sap, and other liquids.

Tiny muscles in the head help pump fluid up through the proboscis for more efficient meals.

The proboscis stays tucked into a coil until suppertime.

The Madagascan moon moth does not have a mouth, so it doesn't feed as an adult. Because of this, it only lives for a couple of days.
The Madagascan moon moth is sometimes called the comet moth for its long tail.

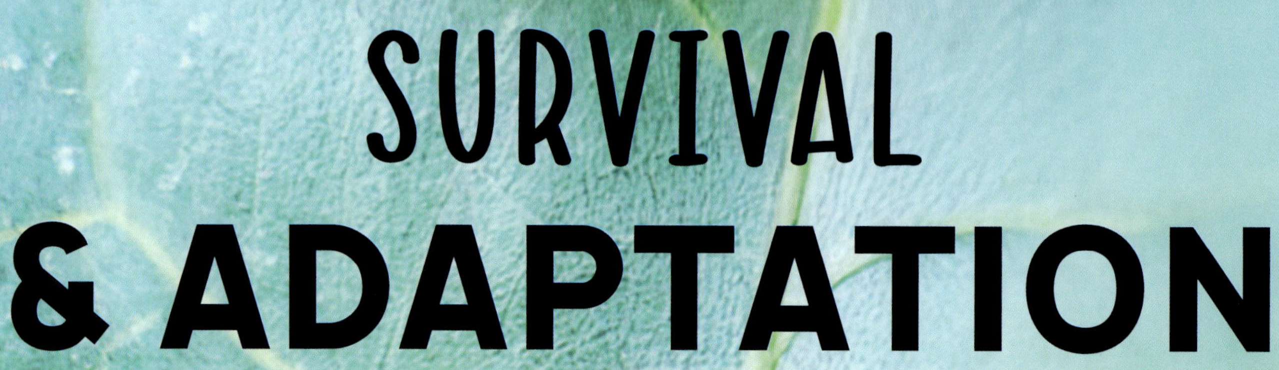

SURVIVAL
& ADAPTATION

Most caterpillars have twelve eyes—six on each side of the head—called ocelli. Among other things, their eyes help the creature detect the movements of potential predators.

Some caterpillars have tiny spines all over their bodies that make them less desirable to predators.

The pipevine swallowtail is poisonous because of the toxins in the plants it eats as a caterpillar. Predators quickly learn to avoid it!

Tiger moths send out ultrasonic clicks to protect themselves from bats. The clicks disorient the bats, who navigate and locate prey by echolocation.

To escape harm and avoid capture, butterflies will sometimes fly in erratic, fluttering patterns.

Some moths and butterflies spray a toxic liquid when threatened—sometimes aimed right at the attacker!

The owl eye spot on a butterfly is an example of mimicry, which is an adaptation that results in one species imitating (or looking like) another to avoid predators or attract prey.

The Indian leaf butterfly has wings that look exactly like a dried leaf, complete with "veins" and spots resembling mold.

Owl butterflies have enormous eye spots on their wings. When the wings are open, the spots mimic an owl's gaze.

Peppered moths are known for their distinct markings that help them blend into trees covered with lichen, which are living organisms consisting of fungus and alga that are beneficial to wildlife.

FLIGHT
TRICKS

Some butterflies, like the painted lady, can survive in scorching desert environments by conserving water and flying long distances to find food.

Some moths, like the hawk moth or hummingbird moth, have streamlined bodies and powerful wings for rapid, agile flight up to 30 mph (48 km/h)!

Hawk moths can hover or even fly backward!

During their annual migration, monarchs travel between 25 and 100 miles (40 and 160 km) a day.

Monarchs migrate up to 2,800 miles (4,506 km) each year using the sun and the Earth's magnetic field to guide them.

Scientists have discovered that moths aren't "attracted" to light. Instead, light disorients them, causing these insects to fly in circles.

Butterflies and moths often vibrate their wings to warm up before taking flight.

Butterfly wings aren't actually colored—they reflect light in specific ways using tiny, overlapping scales.

The Atlas moth has a wingspan of 10 to 12 inches (25 to 30 cm). Its wings are as big as a dinner plate!

Female Atlas moths have a narrower gap between their wings than males.

The Hercules moth has a wingspan that can reach up to 11 inches (28 cm). As a caterpillar, this moth can grow up to 5 inches (13 cm) long.

You can tell a Hercules moth is male from the long, slender tails on its wings. Female Hercules moths do not have tails.

Chapter 2
SPIDERS

Spiders aren't insects—they're arachnids! They may share some traits with insects, but these creepy-crawly creatures are in a class of their own. With nearly three million spiders for every person on Earth, they're everywhere except Antarctica. Whether they are spinning webs, leaping through the air, or ballooning across oceans on strands of silk, spiders are nature's ultimate hunters. Turn the page to learn about them!

SPIDER
BASICS

A spider's body has two main parts: the cephalothorax, where the head and legs attach, and the abdomen, which produces silk.

Spiders have eight legs and an even number of eyes—usually eight in total!

All spiders spin silk. It comes from seven special glands and is released through tiny structures in the abdomen called spinnerets.

Spider silk is super stretchy. It can expand up to five times its original length and stay intact!

A purseweb spider builds a tube out of silk. Then it waits inside. When an insect gets too close, the spider cuts through the tube, grabs the insect, and pulls it inside. Snack time!

An orb web looks like a wagon wheel. The spider spins the web in a spiral shape. Once constructed, the spider waits for an insect to fly into the sticky trap.

Sheet webs look like a silky hammock across grass or low bushes. Spiders build these as netting to catch insects that fall from trees. Sheet webs are often seen in the morning.

Spiders use webs to help catch their dinner of insects, wrapping prey into snack-sized bundles.

Some spiders line their homes with silk for protection.

Spider silk is super strong for its weight. Some webs are up to five times stronger than steel of the same diameter!

Spiders leave a silk line that leads back to their home when they go wandering to keep them from getting lost.
Spiders will spin silk lifelines to help them escape from predators.
Spiders can "tune" their webs like the strings of a guitar. They adjust the tension of the silk lines to help them detect the movement of prey.

SMART & SNEAKY

Spiders are clever engineers. They create sticky parts of their webs to catch prey, but they're careful to walk only on the non-sticky strands using tiny claws on their feet to grip the silk. This keeps the spider from getting caught in its own trap!

Jumping spiders are acrobats! They can leap several inches to ambush prey or escape danger. With amazing vision from their four pairs of eyes, they're the ninjas of the spider world.

Wolf spiders don't wait for dinner—they chase down their prey like furry hunters on eight legs!

SMALL EYES, BIG BODIES

The Goliath birdeater tarantula can grow up to 12 inches (30 cm) wide and weigh as much as 6 ounces (170 g)—about the size of a small dinner plate! Despite its name, this creature rarely, if ever, eats birds. It mostly feeds on arthropods, worms, and the occasional amphibian.

The giant huntsman spider is found in Laos. It has crablike legs, with a leg span of up to 12 inches (30 cm), making it one of the world's largest spiders.

The King Baboon Tarantula uses its strength to burrow and defend its territory.

BABY SPIDERS

Female spiders create little beds of silk in which to safely place their eggs. They then spin another silk sac around the eggs to protect them.

Baby spiders are called spiderlings.

When they are ready to leave their moms, spiderlings climb somewhere high and tilt their abdomens up so the wind catches their silk. They then ride the silk line as it travels through the air. This is called "ballooning."

Instead of depositing her eggs in a silk sac, wolf spider moms carry their eggs with them. When the eggs hatch, her spiderlings ride on top of her back until they are big enough to leave.

VENOMOUS SPIDERS

Not all spiders are dangerous, but some—like the black widow and the brown recluse—pack a venomous punch. Black widow bites can cause muscle pain, while the brown recluse's venom can destroy tissue around the bite.

Spiders don't chew—they inject venom through hollow fangs. This venom turns the prey's insides into bug soup, which spiders slurp up with their strawlike mouths. Yum!

Some spiders spit! Instead of injecting venom—a gooey, sticky liquid—they will spit it on their prey, which prevents their victim from leaving.

Spider fangs don't stop at injecting venom—some species use their fangs for handy purposes, such as digging burrows or carrying prey.

Chapter 3
BEETLES

Beetles have been around since prehistoric times. They even survived the mass extinction that wiped out the dinosaurs. Tough and full of surprises, beetles can glow, make noise, fly, destroy crops—and sometimes even save them. They come in a variety of shapes, sizes, and colors. They eat pests, clean up waste, and pollinate flowers, making them important to the Earth's ecosystem. Let's meet these fascinating little creatures.

BEETLE
BASICS

There are more than 400,000 species of beetle around the world—about the population of Tulsa, Oklahoma!—and many more not yet identified.

One out of every four animals on Earth is a beetle. Put another way, this means that 25 percent of all Earth's creatures are beetles.

Beetles live almost everywhere: deserts, rainforests, beaches, and mountains.

The rose chafer is a member of the scarab family of beetles. Its uniquely colored shell is iridescent green and bronze.

Depending on the species, a beetle's lifespan is anywhere from a few days to a few years.

Beetles' tough, armorlike shells, called elytra, are made of chitin, which protects them from predators and extreme weather.

Some beetles can fly. They open their delicate wings from underneath their tough, shell-like exterior when they want to take off.

RHINOCEROS
BEETLES

This small but mighty beetle can lift more than eight hundred times its body weight. It's considered one of the strongest insects around.

Males use their horns to fight off predators. They also use them to square off with other rhino beetles when competing for the attention of a female mate.

These beetles use their horns as mini excavators. They dig themselves into the ground for protection.

DUNG BEETLES

By cleaning up droppings, dung beetles recycle nutrients into the soil, keeping the environment healthy and clean.

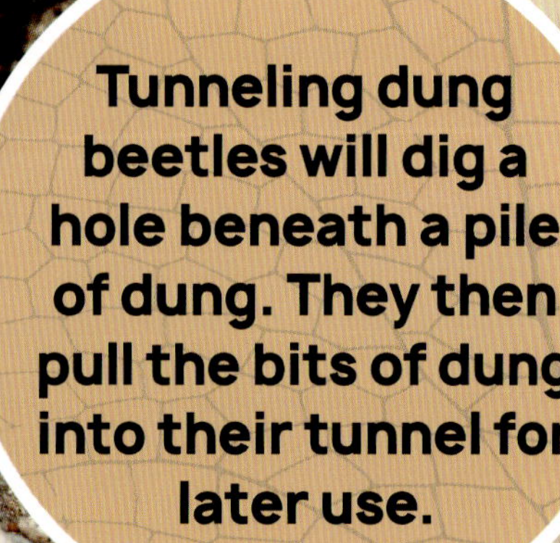

Tunneling dung beetles will dig a hole beneath a pile of dung. They then pull the bits of dung into their tunnel for later use.

Some dung beetles shape animal droppings into balls. The beetles then roll the dung away to be used as a food source for them and their babies.

A dung beetle can roll a ball fifty times its own weight—the equivalent of a child pulling a car!

Dweller dung beetles live inside animal dung. Females lay their eggs so when their larvae hatch, they are able to enjoy a ready-made meal. Yum!

LADYBUG BEETLES

There are more than six thousand species of ladybug in the world, four hundred fifty of which live in North America.

Sometimes, a ladybug will pretend to be dead to protect itself against a predator.

In addition to eating soft-bodied insects, some ladybugs feed on fungi and plants.

When threatened, some ladybugs release a stinky liquid from their legs. It's their way of warding off predators.

Ladybugs come in various colors: red, yellow, orange, blue, pink, and even black and white. Some ladybugs don't have any spots at all. These are called spotless lady beetles.

A single ladybug can eat up to five thousand aphids (tiny plant-eating insects) in its lifetime.

Ladybugs live to be only about a year old, which means that one month for a ladybug is equivalent to about seven human years!

FIREFLY
BEETLES

Fireflies don't have long to shine—adults live only about two months, just enough time to mate and lay eggs.

Fireflies snack on worms and snails before they develop their glow feature.

Most of their lives are spent as larvae.

Fireflies, or lightning bugs, are soft-bodied beetles that light up warm summer nights with their glowing tails. This trait is called bioluminescence.

Bioluminescence helps beetles attract mates through blinking patterns unique to their species.

A firefly's glow warns predators that it tastes bad.

BEASTLY BEETLES

The Hercules beetle, named after the legendary strongman, can grow up to 7 inches (18 cm) long, including its horn.

Native to Africa, the Goliath beetle is as big as a small apple. It grows to 4.5 inches (11.4 cm) long.

The Titan beetle from South America reaches nearly 7 inches (18 cm) in length—as long as a smartphone! Despite their size, these gentle giants mostly feed on rotting wood and pose no threat to humans.

Chapter 4
FLIES

Flies might seem like pesky buzzers (and they're not too fun at picnics!), but they're some of the most fascinating and important creatures on Earth. They can beat their wings more than two hundred times per second. They're also able to flip, roll, and spin in the air, which is why they're so hard to catch! With super senses and incredible adaptability, these insects are built for survival.

SUPER FLY
FACTS

As a food source for birds, spiders, and other animals, flies and mosquitoes in general are an important part of the food chain.

Mosquitoes are a type of fly. Their larvae grow in water and provide food for fish, frogs, and other animals.

Flies keep ecosystems healthy. They eat dead animals, rotting plants, and other decaying material, acting as tiny recyclers. Without flies, waste would pile up.

Houseflies can taste what they land on thanks to little sensors in their feet that double as taste buds.

The lifespan of an average housefly is fifteen to twenty-eight days. They reproduce quickly to ensure their populations thrive.

Houseflies and hoverflies sip liquids like nectar, tree sap, or fruit juice.

Flies are a key pollinator of cacao, which is used to make chocolate. Some plants wouldn't grow without flies to pollinate them.

Flies don't have teeth, so they can't chew. Instead, enzymes in their saliva turn solids into liquids, which allow them to consume their food.

Mosquitoes, horseflies, and deer flies rely on blood meals for survival. They have long, needlelike mouthparts that pierce skin and allow them to access blood vessels.

MASTERS OF ADAPTATION

Flies are some of the most adaptable creatures on the planet. This means they can easily respond to changing environmental conditions to protect themselves.

Hoverflies are a type of bee lookalike, but they don't sting. They only mimic a bee to avoid predators.

Stalk-eyed flies inflate their eye stalks to impress mates. It's like having built-in sunglasses!

The bumblebee robber fly disguises itself as a bumblebee to avoid predators while using its sharp proboscis to catch prey for itself.

Crane flies are harmless giants that look like mosquitoes to help protect themselves against predators.

WEIRD & WONDERFUL SUPERPOWERS

Flies can hover, change direction midair, and even fly backward, making them master fliers that are hard to swat and nearly impossible to catch.

Some flies produce silk threads to anchor themselves. They are one of the few insects besides spiders that can do this.

Unlike most common flies, horseflies have a painful bite.

Studies of fruit flies have helped scientists understand genetic disorders like cancer, Alzheimer's disease, Parkinson's disease, and muscular dystrophy by modeling how mutations affect cells and tissues.

Flies have compound eyes that contain thousands of lenses, which means a fly can see almost everything around it, including small movements far away. Their eyes help them detect and avoid danger.

Blowflies are often the first to arrive at a decomposing body. This helps forensic scientists estimate time of death.

DANGEROUS & DEADLY
MOSQUITOES

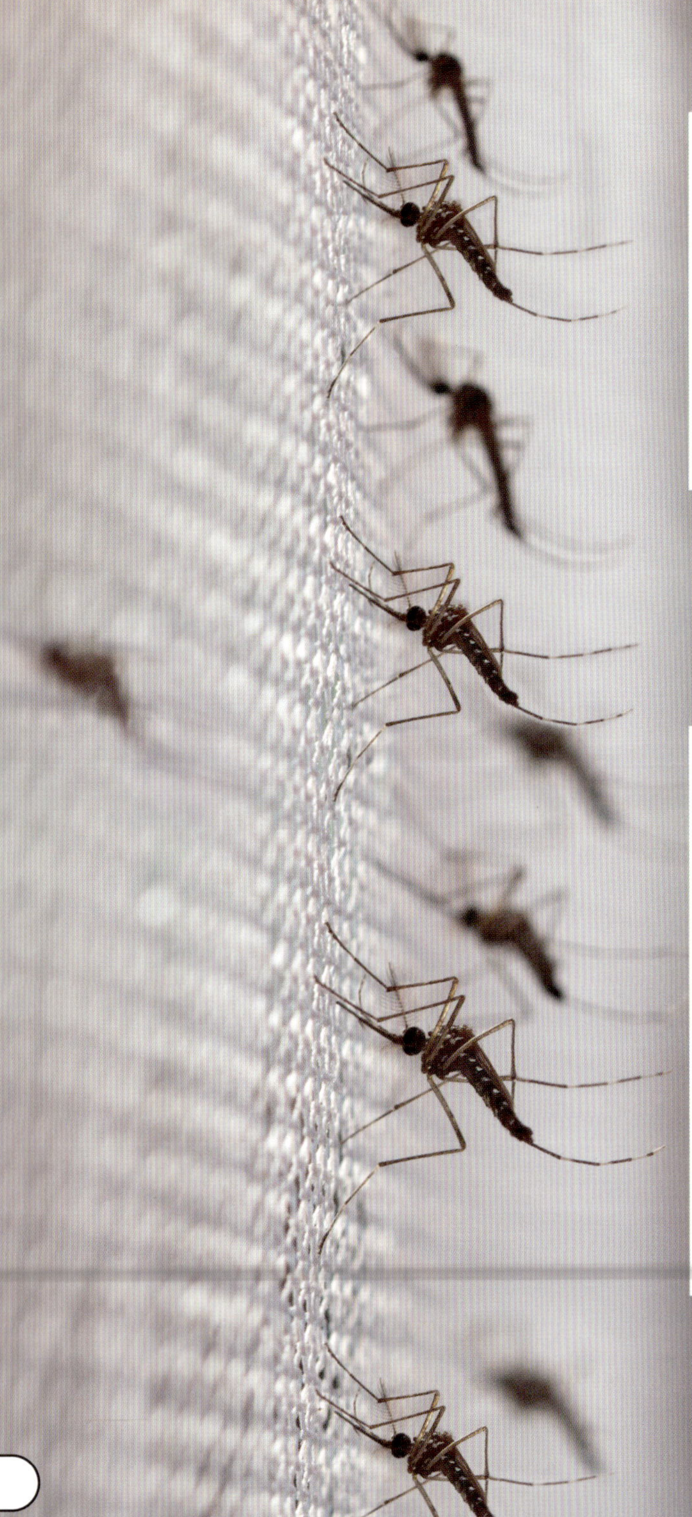

Mosquitoes are responsible for spreading diseases like malaria, dengue fever, and Zika virus, making them some of the deadliest creatures on the planet.

Mosquito-borne diseases affect people all over the world, especially in warm, tropical areas where mosquitoes thrive. Scientists and health professionals work hard to fight these diseases using mosquito nets, sprays, and even natural predators.

Scientists continue to study these tiny creatures to find better ways to limit their spread of disease.

Applying a spray repellent to the skin can help protect the body against mosquito bites.

Female mosquitoes need blood to lay their eggs. When they bite, they can pick up germs, like viruses and parasites, passing them from one person or animal to another. Males do not feed on blood and instead drink nectar or don't feed at all.

Chapter 5

WASPS, ANTS & BEES

As some of the hardest-working insects around, wasps, bees, and ants are nature's tiny superheroes! Bees are champion pollinators, while wasps and ants help control pests and recycle nutrients. Many of these insects live in highly organized colonies, working together in teams. They're found nearly everywhere on Earth, and they're always busy doing amazing things for our planet. Let's take a closer look!

BUSY BEE
BASICS

Bees help plants grow fruits and flowers through pollination, which is the process of moving pollen from one plant or flower to another to help them reproduce.
More than twenty thousand species of bee exist around the world.
Without bees to pollinate them, many plants and flowers would die and become extinct, which would have a global impact on food production.

Megachile bees are solitary and live in their own nests without workers or a queen.
Megachile pluto, or Wallace's giant bee, is the world's largest bee. It can grow up to nearly 2 inches (5 cm) long—about the size of a walnut.

The world's tiniest bee is Perdita minima. It's smaller than a grain of rice.
Leaf-cutter bees can carry leaves that are larger than their bodies. They use leaves to pad their nests.
Not all bees look alike. Some are black and yellow, while others shimmer in metallic green or purple. Some bees are smooth, while others are fuzzy.

HARDWORKING HONEYBEES

Worker bees are females who clean the hive, care for the queen and babies, build honeycombs, collect nectar, make honey, and defend the hive.

Male bees, or drones, have one job—to mate with a queen from another hive. Afterward, their short lives come to an end.

The queen bee lays up to two thousand eggs a day and releases special chemicals to keep the hive running smoothly.
Honeybees are social insects that live in huge, organized hives where everyone has a job.

WONDROUS WASPS

Wasps are omnivores. Much of their diet consists of other insects, such as caterpillars and flies.

Wasps are a diverse group of insects with more than 100,000 known species. There are likely many more to be discovered.

Parasitic wasps lay eggs inside living hosts. The larvae feed on their host, keeping pest populations in check.

While many wasps live alone, species like hornets and yellow jackets form colonies.

Jewel wasps inject venom into cockroaches, turning them into mind-controlled zombies. The wasp lays eggs on the roach, and the larvae eat it alive. Gross!

AGILE & ATTENTIVE
ANTS

Like other insects, the ant has an exoskeleton, which means the outside of its body is hard.

For every human on Earth, there are about 2.5 million ants! There are more than twelve thousand ant species—and probably many more, according to scientists.

Some ants and aphids are friends! Ants protect aphids from predators in exchange for access to the aphids' sweet honeydew secretions.

Ants are social and experts in teamwork. They work together to move leaves, twigs, and other items they need.

Ants can lift more than fifty times their body weight. Trap-jaw ants are especially impressive—they can snap their powerful jaws shut at a speed of 140 mph (225 km/h).

Ants will carry dead ants away from the nest to protect it from predators. Some ants even bury their dead.

ANT
COLONIES

Ant nests can be underground or above ground. As ants dig underground, they create the anthills that are visible above ground. Underground nests can go as deep as 20 feet (6 m) and contain tunnels and rooms for designated purposes.

Ants build colonies that contain millions of individuals, including a queen, workers, and soldiers to defend the nest.

Chapter 6

WOOD-FEEDING BUGS

Wood-feeding bugs may be tiny, but they can cause big, big trouble! These insects, mites, and other arthropods damage trees by boring into bark, sucking sap, or spreading diseases. They don't stop at trees—some even invade homes, feasting on wooden walls and furniture. Let's uncover their fascinating and sometimes creepy world.

TERMITE TROUBLE

Termites chew through wood to eat cellulose, the tough material in plant cell walls.

Even though termites are often considered pests, they help recycle nutrients in forests by breaking down dead trees.

Termites live in massive colonies with millions of members, including workers, soldiers, and a queen, who lays thousands of eggs daily.
Some termites in Africa and Australia build towering mud mounds over 10 feet (3.05 m) tall, complete with "air conditioning" holes to keep their nests cool.

BARK BEETLES

Some bark beetles carry fungi that spread diseases to trees. These pests have destroyed millions of acres of forests across North America.

At 0.125 inches (0.32 cm) long, bark beetles are teeny—only about the size of a ballpoint pen tip.

PRETTY, BUT PESKY

The emerald ash borer is a green shiny beetle that has destroyed millions of ash trees in North America.

The emerald ash borer is an invasive pest native to Asia and Russia. It arrived in North America in the early 2000s, probably by hitching rides aboard cargo ships.

Longhorn beetles produce wood-boring larvae. Some longhorn beetles have antennae as long as, or longer than, their bodies.

Longhorn beetles live for only about forty days.

FUNGI
FEEDERS

Ambrosia beetles live in wood, but they feed on fungi. As a result, they spread fungal spores to trees.

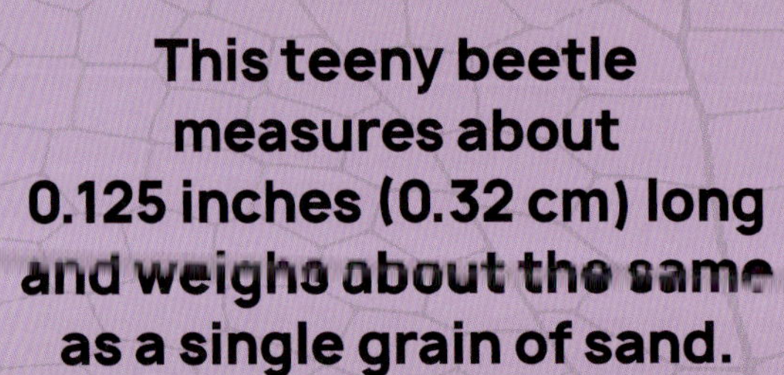

This teeny beetle measures about 0.125 inches (0.32 cm) long and weighs about the same as a single grain of sand.

Although fungi are
a tasty meal for
ambrosia beetles,
the fungi prevent the
tree from absorbing
water, which it needs
to survive.

TINY TROUBLE

Spider mites are so tiny that you need a magnifying glass to see them.

Natural predators like ladybugs help control the number of spider mites, which can damage trees, gardens, and plants.

These tiny arachnids thrive in hot, dry weather and can multiply quickly. A single female can lay hundreds of eggs, creating an army in no time.

PROTECTING TREES & FORESTS

In the wild, scientists use natural predators like parasitic wasps and predators like beetles to fight harmful bugs in forests.

Trees help sustain life on Earth, which is why it's important to protect them. Preserving trees and forests helps ensure a healthy ecosystem for generations to come.

Watering, fertilizing, and generally caring for backyard trees can help prevent pesky bug infestations.
Forest workers sometimes treat trees with special chemicals to repel pests or stop infestations.

Chapter 7
RARE INSECTS

There are millions of insects around the world, and they live in nearly every type of biome, or natural habitat. Some are rare or hard to find, while others are in danger of extinction from habitat loss and climate change. Protecting biodiversity means protecting rare insects and the balance of nature that keeps our planet healthy. In this chapter, we'll highlight some rare and fascinating insects.

BUTTERFLY BEAUTIES

Found only in Papua New Guinea, the Queen Alexandra's birdwing is the largest butterfly in the world, with a wingspan of up to 11 inches (28 cm).

Leona's little blue is a non-migratory butterfly discovered in 1991 in Oregon, USA. It lives on buckwheat nectar and lays eggs only on buckwheat leaves native to the area.

The blue morpho butterfly lives in tropical forests. Its lifespan is about 115 days.

Its wingspan measures 5 to 8 inches (13 to 20 cm).

Native to Washington, USA, the Island Marble butterfly was believed extinct, until it was seen in 1998.

DRAGONFLIES & DAMSELFLIES

The Hine's Emerald dragonfly is an indicator species—its presence means the ecosystem is healthy. A decrease in the population of this species is a sign that an ecosystem is in trouble.

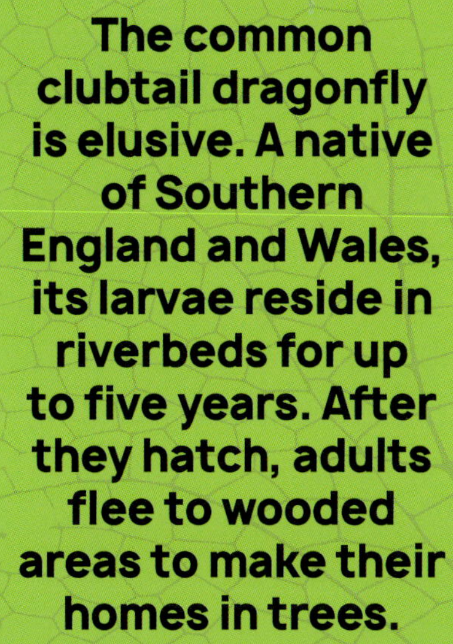

The common clubtail dragonfly is elusive. A native of Southern England and Wales, its larvae reside in riverbeds for up to five years. After they hatch, adults flee to wooded areas to make their homes in trees.

The blue damselfly is a tiny creature with translucent wings. Males are usually blue with black spots, which appear like rings along the length of their bodies.

The San Francisco forktail damselfly is the rarest and smallest of its species in North America. Males come in iridescent shades of black, green, and blue. Females are gold. Its home is in the Presidio of San Francisco, a national park in California.

RARE
BEETLES

The bumblebee scarab beetle has antennae with little plates at each tip. The plates help it smell and detect movement. They can also press into a club or fan out.

The Madagascar giraffe weevil gets its name from its elongated neck.
It is found only in Madagascar rainforests and cloud forests, and it is hard to find in the wild.

Tiger beetles are known by their blue-green color and six yellowish spots.
Their numbers are dwindling in North America due to habitat loss, and many species are endangered.

UNIQUE INSECTS

Native to New Zealand, the giant tree weta is a cricketlike insect that can weigh as much as a sparrow! Its body alone is about 3 inches (8 cm) long.

Known for its courtship dances to help attract mates, the tiny Australian peacock spider can jump more than twenty times the size of its own body.

Walking stick insects have long, thin bodies and legs that look like twigs. They can vanish into the trees to protect themselves.

Leaf insects blend into leaves and plants because they look like them. This makes it hard for predators to find them.

Chapter 8
PROTECTING INSECTS

Have you heard the phrase "save the bees"? It became well known in conservation groups in the early 2000s when it was discovered that bee populations were declining around the globe. Although some bee populations have stabilized, wild bees and many other bugs, insects, and critters remain endangered. It's up to us to learn about these threats so that we can take action to prevent insects from becoming extinct. That's what this chapter is all about.

WHY INSECTS ARE ENDANGERED

Other threats
include air pollution,
pesticide use, and
light pollution from
cities, which can
disrupt the mating
and feeding activities
of nocturnal insects,
such as elephant
hawk moths.

Rising global temperatures and
shifting weather patterns make
it hard for insects to find
food and shelter.

WHAT CAN WE DO?

Create insect hotels. People can build habitats for endangered pollinators in their gardens. Attracting certain insects to your yard or community can help balance the loss of habitats in different areas.

Start a garden. Native plants attract local insects and provide food for them. Flowers encourage bees to pollinate.
Support conservation groups to help protect insects' habitats. Planting trees, volunteering to pick up litter in nature areas, and being respectful of insects and wildlife are just some ways to help.
Make a compost bin to attract soldier flies, worms, and other critters to break down organic materials into nutrient-rich soil that can be used in a garden.

GLOSSARY

adaptable: able to adjust to new environments

Alzheimer's disease: a condition in which the memory and thinking skills decline over time

antennae: sensory appendage on an insect's head that allows them to touch, hear, taste, and smell, as well as navigate their surroundings and detect danger

arachnids: a group of animals that have eight legs. This includes spiders, scorpions, and ticks.

aphids: tiny bugs that suck juice out of plants, often damaging them

ballooning: when some small creatures, like spiders, deploy silk threads to "catch" the wind and travel through the air

bioluminescence: the ability for some living things to make their own light

biome: a large area of the world in which living things share a similar environment

cellulose: a basic structural component of plant cell walls that helps keep the plants strong

cephalothorax: a body part in spiders that consists of both the head and middle section, which are fused together

cocoon: a stiff covering spun from silk that protects a caterpillar while it changes into a moth

chitin: a naturally occurring substance that helps form the exoskeleton and hardened exteriors of some insects

chrysalis: the hard, shell-like exterior that protects a caterpillar while it changes into a butterfly

echolocation: the ability to locate objects through reflected sound waves

ecosystem: a community of organisms in an environment that functions as a single ecological unit; for example, the forest and the ocean are both ecosystems

endangered: when an animal and/or plant is in danger of disappearing from the world

extinct: when an animal, insect, plant, or other organism ceases to exist

fertilizing: a process in which nutrients are added to plants so they can grow

fungi: organisms like mushrooms or mold that live on plants, animals, or decaying things

germs: small organisms that can make people sick

infestations: a pest population, such as mice or bugs, in a specific location causing problems and/or damage to that environment

iridescent: a rainbowlike color display that shimmers and appears to change when viewed from different angles

larvae: the early stage of some insects before they grow into adults

mosquito-borne illness: diseases that are spread by mosquitoes, such as Zika virus and malaria

muscular dystrophy: a condition that weakens muscles, making it hard to move over time

nectar: a sweet liquid secreted by plants that is often consumed as a food source by bugs and insects

ocelli: simple eyes found on insects that help them detect light

omnivore: an animal or organism that eats from multiple food sources, such as plants, animals, algae, and fungi.

Parkinson's disease: a progressive disease that affects the brain, disrupting movement, balance, and coordination

pheromone: a special chemical that animals use to communicate with each other

pollination: the process where pollen from one flower moves to another flower, helping plants grow seeds

pollinators: animals, like bees, that help flowers and plants make seeds by spreading pollen

predator: an animal or organism that preys on another animal or organism

proboscis: a long, tubelike mouth part that helps animals suck up nectar and food

scorching: very hot or burning

setae: tiny hairs or bristles on animals, like insects, that help them feel or grip things

spiderlings: baby spiders

spinnerets: structures in a spider's abdomen that produce silk for webs and silk lines

ultrasonic: sounds that are too high-pitched for humans to hear, but some animals, like bats, can hear them

venom: a toxic substance used by animals to help protect themselves or to catch prey

PHOTO CREDITS

COVER: Wirestock Creators (top left), Kurit afshen (top middle), LedyX (top right), inlovepai (main).
INTERIOR: Images courtesy of Shutterstock, except marble island butterfly image on page 95, courtesy of USFWS. **Page 2:** LedyX (top), Eric Isselee (left), Irin-k (bottom), New Africa (right). **Page 3:** irin-k (top). **Page 4:** Gan Chaonan (top), Wirestock Creators (middle), Protasov AN (bottom left and bottom right). **Page 5:** Protasov AN. **Page 6:** Kriachko Oleksii. **Page 8:** Kim Howell. **Page 9:** Sari Oneal (top, bottom), Fiona M. Donnelly (second from top), Manuel Balesteri (third from top). **Page 10:** Anatoliy Berislavskiy (left), Catocala7 (right). **Page 11:** BlueDiamond86 (top left), Wirestock Creators (top right), Robert Sanjeev Ross (bottom left), guraydere (bottom right). **Page 12:** Dark Moon Pictures. **Page 13:** SilviaClarisaZaninovich (top), Ian Sap (middle), Bulinko (bottom). **Page 14:** Eduard Andrica (top), Cornel Constantin (bottom). **Page 15:** Andreas Weitzmann. **Page 16:** grafisio. **Page 17:** James W. Thompson (top), Lima_84 (middle), Darkdiamond67 (bottom). **Page 18:** Mountainpix. **Page 19:** golfza.357 (top), Vladfotograf (middle), Marek R. Swadzba (bottom). **Page 20:** Marek Mierzejewski. **Page 21:** JHVEPhoto (main), aaltair (inset). **Page 22:** MrKotov (top), Cornel Constantin (bottom). **Page 23:** Akarawut (top), ChameleonsEye (bottom). **Page 24:** DimaSid. **Page 26:** Leoniek van der Vliet. **Page 27:** Ervin Herman (top), Tacio Philip Sansonovski (middle), Valeriy Karpeev (bottom). **Page 28:** Eduardo Dzophoto. **Page 29:** Lancan (top), Rix Pix Photography (middle), Stephen Farhall (bottom). **Page 30–31:** CeltStudio. **Page 32:** Maaike van der Toom (top), Lukas Zdrazil (middle), Vinicius R. Souza (bottom). **Page 33:** reptiles4all (top), iSKYDANCER (middle), Lucian Coman (bottom). **Page 34–35:** Levent Konuk (main). **Page 35:** Sean McVey (top). **Page 36:** Ernie Cooper. **Page 37:** guraydere (top), Katarina Christenson (bottom). **Page 38:** Nurdaedin. **Page 40:** Macronatura.es. **Page 41:** LaSvitlana (main), Doni Kirana (inset). **Page 42:** Suwat wongkham. **Page 43:** ruiruito (top), Lightboxx (middle), Mark Brandon (bottom). **Page 44:** Four Oaks. **Page 45:** Andries Combrinck (top), bwagner99 (bottom left), Hein Myers Photography (bottom right). **Page 46:** superoke. **Page 47:** L-N (top), Szabadi Jeno Tibor (middle), gsdm (bottom). **Page 48:** Japan's Fireworks. **Page 49:** WUT.ANUNAI (top), Japan's Fireworks (middle), Stock story (bottom). **Page 50:** Ocskay Mark. **Page 51:** Rammy_Rammy (top), PetlinDmitry (middle), guentermanaus (bottom). **Page 52:** Young Swee Ming. **Page 54:** Vova Shevchuk. **Page 55:** Pedro Turrini Neto (top), Enid Versfeld (bottom). **Page 56–57:** nechaevkon (main). **Page 56:** Liew Weng Keong (top), Narong Khueankaew (bottom). **Page 57:** weerapongss (inset).